WORDS UNSPOKEN

QUOTES AND POEMS

SMITA BUXI

ISBN 979-888569872-6

This book is dedicated to my IDEAL whom I have followed always and of course to my two daughters, perhaps because these girls only have understood my expressions better than any one else. My daughters have been a source of tremendous encouragement. Ever since they have grown up!

Contents

Contents

Contents

Contents

Preface

The intricacies of human behaviour can never be measured by anyone. I believe, a sensitive mind and a clear perception of the surroundings may express to some extent the various responses to human actions. In one such phase of my life, I began treading on this path when I came across several human emotions such as pain and sufferings that every common person has to go through. My book 'WORDS UNSPOKEN' contains various expressions of thoughts, ideas, perceptions, sometimes direct, at times indirect as a mere observer. After hardships there is a definite glow of rewards showered by the Almighty on each and every human being. My faith in God and in the beauties of Nature have acted as a refuge for me during the traumas of my life. This made me rise from the debri and rejuvenate myself with motivational rays. This book is replete with shades of pain as well as much brighter shades of overcoming the pain and rising with joy and exhilaration. The book aims to convey these expressions to many readers who too have gone through this rough and rewarding terrain of human experiences.

Prologue

I started writing poems and short quotes first on YourQuote writing app. Earlier my knack for writing was mainly in my own personal diaries. This app gave me a boost to make my words reach to many people around the world. I am thankful to my followers for appreciating my works. This book is basically a conglomeration of various poems and quotes that I have been expressing on YourQuote since past three years. Hope you all will be able to connect with this collection!

POEMS

Here, you will find a beautiful collection of all sorts of poems, that will stir your heart.

I believe these words as you read on will certainly make you feel closer to your real life experiences.

- SMITA BUXI

Motherland

Where freedom reigns high ,

and many hearts dance with joy,

where deeds of valour leave,

their imprints on young minds,

where lush green valleys and meadows,

take me on a ride to heaven,

there I find solace amidst the strife.

Where God is worshipped like,

on no other land,

there I discover my own Motherland.

Capture the universe

Wandering alone on a lonely night,

under the starry sky I want,

to capture this majestic beauty,

filling the vast expanse as if,

in a dream , yet so real that ,

I can't but marvel, awe struck ,

as I yearn to be lost, as soon as

I capture, the universe in my heart.

A Question

Life is a question,

an unanswered question;

despite a thousand self-introspection,

and a manifold ways of inspection,

with many stories of resurrection,

of man and his tireless liberation,

remains a painful question.

Crowning Beauty

We shall overcome sooner or later,

we shall walk together sooner than later,

in pursuit of peace far from the world of malice .

We shall march with a fiery siege of

those who dare put us down and bestow love and wisdom

sapped from earth, that this world once again,

in the name of God becomes a crowning beauty .

Tears of hurt

Let your tears flow

even if they can't pierce

someone's stony heart

like an arrow,

just let them flow and flow.

One day shall they move

the earth and the sky and

break the wall of that stinking ice ,

that caused your tears to flow.

Winds of change

In the blue hour I sit under ,

the bright halo in wait for,

the flute of love that would pour into

many a wounded hearts ,

a thousand melodies of changing harps.

This time the wind will blow ,

not for you not for me but,

for the whole of suffering lot,

who tremble in dread of callous hands ,

that got them baked in terrible heat,

of their sheer power, lust and greed.

,

The dark and the light

The stairs of loneliness,

pulling down to forgetfulness

into the distant dark corridors

of the heart's chambers,

will never bring peace

to the soul in need.

***Light** the light of wisdom ,*

no matter if its seldom,

ushering in, a calm,

driving away the pain as a balm,

and make this eventful life a witness

to a feeble bird flying from her nest.

Memories

I cherish

your memories ,embedded

deep within,

whenever I happen to feel

your presence,

in soft and tender whisperings ,

coming through

these thick and thorny woods,

where in ,

I often search my lost strings.

Don't ask

Never ask ever

the ocean

why its so clear

and blue and transparent,

an eye of beautiful nature;

dive rather, into

its crystal water,

and seek for your answer

resting cool , hidden under .

Stage called life

Amidst the glow of bright lights,

of ambition and temptation,

we step in, to perform,

as best as we can ;

and within the time allotted,

we keep going ahead,

with a burning desire to be applauded .

It so happens that,

we tend to commit blunders,

that shake us to hilt,

and the stage of life then,

seems so dim lighted,

yet the hankering soul ,

wants even more to be applauded.

Rise and bloom

To forget your pain ,

stand in the rain,

and the heavenly showers,

shall help you gain,

your hidden powers.

One day will shine the sun,

into your dark room,

under the sparkling rays soon,

your heart shall bloom.

She

She wore the anklets

and danced upon the stage ,

of vast, dark universe ,

till the earth and the sky ,

had burst into applause !

Amidst dust and dirt ,

lay the broken space ,

tattered and shattered ,

when mercy! and more mercy !

cries rend the air.

Below in the fields of hope,

little droplets of mercy,

shed in showers of rain,

turn the wounds into ,

some muddy patches ,

and out sprout the saplings !!

Lost sheep

Time is ripe for a deep ponder;

ye lost sheep! step out of slumber.

Strike the cord of thought ,

and wonder ;

who are you , that you don't remember.

Some deeds of worth , your own forefather,

had imbued in you and you dare to plunder ?

Time and again the cosmic flame,

will rise like thunder,

to cleanse us all above and under,

until we learn to ponder and wonder.

A bird's cry

As I lay on the golden sand,

close to my beloved,

there in my heart,

while gazing at the glittering stars,

over the black velvet sheet above,

I heard a bird cry, in the quiet night dry;

Far from some distant land ,

perhaps huddled in a nest,

her cries never allowed me any rest!

My journey

Under the star studded roof,

through shadows of the dark,

I steer my journey into the beyond,

into the grandeur of some foreign land.

I travel across a thousand towns,

holding on to few helping hands,

and marvel the images of human panorama,

dipped in coatings of sweet and sour.

Sounds of silence

The day is over, twilight is here,

sooner, not later,

we all shall hear,

sounds of silence, loud and clear,

in each nook and corner,

you hold so dear,

until you discard your dread and fear,

and adopt Faith, the arrow in your armour.

Me and Mind

Once the fight gets over,

between me and my mind,

certainly a big tight embrace ,

of some heavenly kind,

shall touch my sesnses and

would draw a line ,

and leave me solely ,

for Thee and Thine.

The rhyme of 'Nothing'

Nothing in life,

that we yearn for,

can ever be permanent.

Nothing comes easy,

that we sit and wait.

Nothing stays with you

that you take as yours.

Nothing waits for you,

as change is the law.

Nothing comes to you,

if you don't go to them.

Nothing can harm you,

if you don't harm any.

Nothing can shake you ,

if your faith is unshaken.

The little flame

Like a shooting star,

you stepped into my small world;

shone like diamond in thousands

and so you became my own world.

My *little flame,*

I beseech thee thus, stop not thy burning,

till my efforts are on

to refuel thy lighting,

with love for God and thy yearning .

The rigid past

Missing those moments

when life seems still,

calm, serene as,

the cold winter stream,

when time peeps in,

probing my thoughts,

when memories of past,

come rushing in a gust,

refuses to leave as,

the rigid rust .

The divine beauty

Gazing across the meadows,

through weeds and grass,

dancing , tickling rays ,

enliven my senses,

as I drink the beauty,

wrapt in such divinity.

Let me collect O'scented flower beds,

few lovely hues of nature,

for offerings at the altar.

O' *let me pass through these*

bright pathways and bring home

a handful, for my dark alleyways.

The sun

The sun knows

you

your hidden interiors

which you have covered

with darkness around

you.

Let it in

allow the glory to pervade

and melt the layers of

ignorance and guilt, O' just

let it in.

True love

A windfall of love , a rare virtue,

unseen in this corporeal frame,

of flesh and blood ,

may still be sought

into the higher realms

that comprises of ,

sanctity of true relationships ,

and yet can fulfill

the heart's unfulfilled expectations.

Dream

Lost as she was in her own

thoughts,

lady luck some day may smile

at her perhaps,

hoping against hope,

for hours

in the dusk she strolled,

when the sky went dark

and out came the stars.

The dream she had seen made her

to wonder;

will there be a home of her choice ,

couldn't but murmur,

for, the symbols in the dream, had come

to so deliver.

The headmaster

Winter tiptoes into the homes,

as a hard headed headmaster,

wielding his stick of icy winds,

pushes us in, under warm blankets.

He keeps guard on our outings,

and seems happy at our cold shiverings;

when in cold chilly winds we tremble,

how we hear his laughter crackle!

To young hearts

An old heart longs to speak volumes,

to many a young hearts,

of the lost lost world ,

that is alive but, in narrow lanes,

of long forgotten culture,

and values and tradition,

of those glorious past days, of golden era,

where the traces do carry,

treasures of time dazzling ,

like bounty for the young budding aspirations.

Fear or courage

Let go of all that inflicts and hurts,

be it fear or some sudden surge ,

of insecurity within your own four walls;

believe, you are a human power above

a thousand entities, on earth,

and if, at all you want refuge

from dread and dearth,

seek for, in your own secluded corner,

where resides your God,

who loves to extend His Hand

to every true warrior, fighting on His land.

A prayer

Pray God that ,

He be more merciful,

forgive our wrongs,

that we be more humble,

and shun our egotism,

that we be more agreeable,

and love Him more,

that we be more beautiful ;

for,

what unfinished business,

that sent you from heaven,

can there be but, to

organise yourselves with,

lessons learnt here,

for the next sojourn.

A new beginning

Let the scars be your

hallmark, your identity

of an unstoppable force,

of will and power,

that gushes in

with an elegance ,

beyond comparison.

A new beginning is

here at your door.

Let it in and

drop your curtain

to embrace the challenge.

A beautiful gift

If you cannot change your past,

forget it for good,

and collect the remnants

of unfulfilled wishes;

convert them into a bouquet,

a well designed gift,

of your determined mind,

for adorning your magnificent present.

When angels dance

A day will come when,

up in the heaven

where pink roses bloom,

the angels will dance

at man's fearless struggle,

amidst bells of doom.

The flowers of hope and joy,

will soon spread fragrance

into which a man's soul,

will seep and sleep

with a rare cognizance.

Voices

Some voices are heard

some are unheard

do lend your ears.

They come from beyond

they loom upon our fate

do lend your ears.

Urging to be heard

urging to be known

do lend your ears.

The voices of our past

the voices of our deeds

do lend your ears.

The Nymph

As the sparkling pearl

in a shell , she lay still,

on the golden beach while,

the glowing rays of sun,

danced on her delicate frame.

The nymph smiled in her dreams,

through half awakened eyes,

that dazzled in love ,

that charmed the serenity

with glimpses of beauty!

Ask God

What are you up to dear God ?

Destruction for some preservation

and securing for next generation ?

No medic is able to see

what we are shown by Thee !

What are your plans dear God?

why such secrecy of your decree,

or is it a judgement that many forsee?

And would you change the world order

a bright new world to usher ?

What have been our flaws O' Lord

in this unfathomable universe,

why can't we be pure from perverse ?

Weak and frail we bow before You,

enlighten the path which goes to You

let not death be proud of a fallen crew !

The address

His address when she found,

after a long weary day,

dead with fatigue, alive with love,

little did she know, he lived

so close, so near her home!

Now when he has gone

she holds his smiling photograph

clasped to her heart

but safe from her tears,

that keeps her from being lost,

alone and shattered as in an inferno!

Your love

Do play with me or,

fumble with my emotions,

I am all yours.

Do caress my soul,

with that glance of Thee,

I bow to your love.

Touch me with your smile,

or discard with indifference,

I plead Thee my dearest,

do never leave me desolate .

Letter to Santa

Another year goes by,

change is so nearby.

O' dear Santa come

flying in our hearts,

gifts or not gifts,

just remove the crusts

of hatred, hard as iron,,

and fill us thus with thirst

for Lord's love on earth.

If this or that

If you blame life for this and that,

what you had asked for, not giving that,

If you curse yourself for this and that,

what you had sought, not getting that,

If you accuse others for this and that,

what you did expect, not seeing that,

If you brood constantly for this and that,

what you had aspired not acquiring that,

You shall make a fool of your own self,

when you don't look within your own shell.

Moonlit night

It's full moon tonight

and I won't sleep till,

I have taken my heart's content,

its soothing light, as I,

lift my face up to it,

the shower of this divine beauty

bathes me all

through and through.

QUOTES

These are short, crisp, pert at times , but perhaps true to

everyone's heart. I feel closer and

more drawn to them whenever I read them out.

Hope the readers too will feel the same.

- SMITA BUXI

1

"*Negate the wrongs give no chance. Time never waits for another glance.*"

"*Beauty in small things is seldom perceived indeed by us, the desperate human beings.*"

"*You are never too old to register your whiteness , amidst the youthful blackness.*"

2

"If sun is a bud let me be a small and tender particle of dust in it."

"Love gives you a soulful aroma where the two bloom in sheer unison as lillies in hills do".

"Only this much is the story of a common man, if the struggle was big or small."

3

"*If you wish to be pert , don't allow your hurt to rule your heart, throw it out like a speck of dirt.*"

"*I became yours , the moment I forgot my "I" and melted in you.*"

"*My painted feathers will fly above the white clouds filling the blue expanse with shades of joy.*"

4

"Concentrate your light on corners least bright where looms misery and fright."

"An act of righteousness is an act of justice be it in defiance or sheer acceptance."

"The cosmic flame will soon create a healing aura the whole world waits to witness."

"No storm can hit you hard as the storm in your mind for its the storm inside that creates a storm outside."

5

*"When hope blooms, our soul expands and holds the universe,
as if to traverse its darkest clouds."*

*"There is no greater agony than days spent in repentance that
could have been, but couldn't be your humble acceptance."*

*"Footfalls of death fall on deaf ears when trumpet of courage is
blown with no fears."*

*"Your achievements can never be an end remember, its a trap
you often fall into, at the end.*

6

"*The best demands you a test that tests you to bring out the best.*"

"*Each step in this realm of life is a lesson learnt to secure the next.*"

"*What binds us together shall secure us forever from dawn to dusk.*"

"*The sun in your mind won't let you wander into the wilderness of weeping humanity.*"

7

"*To fly high, ground your feet well and take the leap of faith that takes you to the sky.*"

"*To deal with my pain I prefer to forget its mine and choose to be silent to ponder over thine.*"

"*No love , no hate dear Lord , as I quietly wait, enters my soul, open Thy Gate.*"

"*My faith carries me through thick and thin only when I stop thinking of a win.*"

"Give love to receive love, spend love to buy love , for, love is not love if, one lives not love."

"You are precious for the GOD who dwells in your heart ; how does it matter if, the world of fakeness does not say so."

9

"The day is over, twilight is here, sooner or later, we all shall hear, sounds of silence loud and clear."

"I'll bloom today not for you , not for me just to show my destiny, see you couldn't stop me from blooming."

"Only a true blessing, remains hidden, as diamond in a heap of suffering."

10

"I often ask the moon, if your phases can't stop you from shining can it so be with mine ?"

"We always choose when we cannot afford to lose."

"Sometimes its all pre- planned and we are mere puppets in a human map destiny has manned."

11

"The more you carry grudges , more shall you fail in mending the broken bridges."

"Promises are not like delicate petals in your garden offered to charm and then maligned when you get over with your malicious plans."

"In a relationship, understanding is simply the cake that keeps increasing your appetite."

12

"Try until you are tired of trying and waiting ; something might be more precious under the piles of efforts you had been putting."

"After a cacophony of stormy days loneliness is a boon everone says."

"In the garden of this beautiful life , choose the flowers of your own choice and let them bloom under the sunshine of compassion and care."

13

"When I fail, I stand up again when I win, I don't stop running."

"I shall be with you, not in your dreams, in your sweet heart rather, a room so cozy, how can I ever leave. ."

"Love didn't require any gift from you, just a glance of satisfaction, amidst a noisy world."

14

"The devil inside me cannot nibble my courage if I make it a friend and teach a lesson for his own transformation."

"Life gives us opportunities to avail only when we drop our ifs and buts."

"My shadow reflects what a wonderful companion I am to my own self."

15

"Our conflicts are not outside, rather they have made , a more comfortable sweet home, out of our own maligned senses, and become a permanent resident of our inside."

"Peace is not in your mind but in your doing."

"Ending things with someone is like tearing your heart apart, inviting time to feed on it through ever flowing waves of unseen future."

"If time could talk , past could easily be forgotten, present be surely be redeemed, future be heartily welcomed, history would not be repeated."

16

"Behold the saga of everlasting pain and wondrous delight, the lonely night holds in her bosom."

"Resist evil rather than forsaking it , fearing the consequences of continued resistance."

"Love is more of metaphysical than physical."

"The secrets of this universe cannot be known unless HE lets us."

17

a"I don't see the end point of the line you have drawn."

"Circumstances cannot take control of my senses."

"Tears of repentance at your HOLY FEET will wipe out, all the sins and shall then bathe in the showers of YOUR bliss."

"If you are callous , I cannot be submissive."

"Think before you speak because the replies are just under your nose."

18

"There is no love lost between a give and take relationship."

"Behold the snowy clouds sailing the vast blue sky, holding each other in an embrace."

"Everyone needs some space to bring about a balance when life gets imbalanced."

"There is zero correlation between a man who throws promises every now and then and a man who makes silent promise to himself."

19

"Hope is like a thin ray of light we can see , no matter how deep is the darkness around us."

"I shall continue to wait at the door of your heart."

"God descends on earth only when it has become a garbage of sins."

"You are so real that I can feel you sinking in my veins with each passing moment."

20

"The seeds of desire are often found embedded deep into our past."

"Multiply your confidence by doing what you are afraid of."

"Faith is invincible, stands hard and firm and well grounded , as does a rock, no matter what !"

"Intimacy to me ,is an earnest relationship of being too close mentally, spiritually and then physically."

21

"Give your wounds time to heal because letting go is easier said than done."

"Its imperative that we be more perceptive than judgemental."

"We are living in the most challenging period of this millenium; the wind blows with an uneasy calm."

"The world you have stepped in is not only black and white ; watch out if your foot is right."

22

"Its your rude indifference to someone's hurt that hurts the
most."

"I meet myself day and night whenever I look into your eyes."

"What better union can there be to see as that of the soul with
the body."

"That which can never be fathomed by a human mind is our
Universe."

23

"Love is not just a heart to heart feeling ,a much beyond concept rather, seems to fill voids, and flows like vibrations of God's eternal sound."

"The higher the struggle , greater the reward."

"Empty homes are more killing than sad music."

"Sometimes words fail to suffice for the intensity of our sufferings ."

"To deeply care , one has to love truly and bear the tantrums without a complaint."

24

"Its hard to remain firm as steel , with not a single crack."

"Honesty is our policy and independence our birthright."

"Life doesn't count your tears nor does it wait for you to hold them back; so swift it is , more than wind, will leave you behind, if you don't collect yourself and catch up with its speed."

"Do never yearn for praises , be numb to abuses, make storms your friend, and run with them as many races."

25

"Gossiping people are difficult to be tackled, so , hold them at a distance before you get poisoned."

"Living life meaningfully is as good as occupying your mind meaningfully."

"There is no set standard of loving and getting loved."

"Sense of belongingness can itself bring a much needed transformation."

26

"Yes, you can build your castle even on the ruins of dead emotions."

"Loneliness is not the solution for a depressed soul, but introspection is."

"You cannot control a human entity by force."

"Its good to love God for mere sake of love than out of fear."

"Every failed attempt sets us free from fearful moments, and motivates for the better and brighter ones."

27

"Our attachment to certain opinions and prejudices is perhaps the subtlest form of our egoism."

"Humanity is still comparatively young than in the bygone ages."

"Open your heart unhesitatingly, design with own hands the key to a happy life."

"Its just fine if you have gone off track, remember you can always make a comeback."

28

"Choose if you are born to live this life or you are living because you are born."

"Happy is the man who lives happily not only with his companions but with himself."

"We can only shape our destiny with patience and wisdom."

"Never cry in self pity , if you really wish to be strong."

"You came into my life like a tall , broad pillar to lean upon ."

"Sometimes I ask the mirror when did it last reflect a person happy."

29

"No matter how the world pulls you , be sure you have a
treasure none can ever take from you."

"Tell the world loud and clear , you are only here, to break the
narrow dogma with your own spear."

"Its sheer waste to brood all the time doing nothing for your
redemption."

"Recognise yourself even before the world does."

30

"There is no transformation in our life that is overnight ."

"Be sure you will get your wings when you are pushed to the edge."

"Its in the light of faith and that of reason, Truth shines like the huge sun."

"We all are skeletons inside the layers of our skin."

"Great minds discuss ideas, even greater ones implement them ."

"An unsatisfied person is the most wretched person on earth."

31

"The more you shout the less will you be heard."

"Beware of brooding habit, its a parasite that dwells upon and devours your soul."

"Change is near and hovering in air, bring it into your courtyard."

"Its a hard hard world , make it soft and cozy with hope and courage."

"Beware of the smiling Satan sitting atop the melting glacier of man's innocence."

32

"No matter how zig zag and rough and long is the journey of
your life , it has to end."

"Life is a playground and players are we, and our actions are
the referee."

"What can I say about you when your whole being is seeped in
tales of your acts."

"Your pride towers over you and you assume it your victory,
only to be lost soon, devoured by your own conscience ."

33

"*A tumultuous mind is like an uncontrollable flooded river inundating its banks.*"

❧❧❧

"*If care was a human, earth would be a kingdom of love.*"

❧❧❧

"*If I had chosen that road I would not have attained those lessons of life , this treacherous one has taught.*"

❧❧❧

"*Let the sparkling rays of sun fall on your face as you pledge adherence to this bright Truth and shun darkness coiled round your heart.*"

❧❧❧

"*Mistakes are lessons we have come upon this earth to learn by heart.*"

"*If pain could speak many smiling faces would disappear into oblivion.*"

"*Human malady sprouts from overloaded circuitry of a weakened consciousness.*"

"*Falsity of human nature is directly proportional to pain and suffering.*"

35

"Blooming isn't easy when hands reach out to nip the buds even before they taste growth."

"Knowledge without wisdom like an empty vessel, can only create an awe but no satisfaction to smile on your brow."

"My darkness found you , who illuminated my whole being till I became spotless in you."

"You cannot beat the heat , generated by SUPREME'S seat; your humble heart will certainly win the feat, though the ignorant shall see defeat."

36

"Do not allow a single dream of yours to linger at a doorway for someone's favour."

"Writing saves you from breaking into pieces due to explosion of thoughts."

"Leaves fall like fear slipping slowly part by part, carried away to unknown spaces, some buried under, as the dead who never return."

"Every common man has the potential to become uncommon."

37

"So much this world yearns for love , so much this yearning as never before."

"I found home in the shelter of your love , I found security in the magic of your utterances."

"There is no parameter so far invented or discovered that could fix the limit of human strength and potential."

'Time is the only judge that never sits for hearing of cases in his court."

38

"Obsession , infatuation and possession are dangerous words in matters of true love."

"We need to burn and churn our soul in the path of Truth."

"If tomorrow is hope today is its glimpse."

"Believe me you will get a lion's share for yourself if you dive deep into the values of history."

"Knife wounds heal faster than a wounded heart."

"No one takes the responsibility of your happiness except you alone."

"Trees make me believe , stormy winds cannot harm us if, our roots are firm and well grounded."

"I begin from you , I end on you."

"I think courage lies in standing firm with one who is right but leaving unhesitatingly when he indulges in wrongs."

"Your popularity does not guarantee your righteousness."

40

"Watch out ! we are living in a society where too many wolves roam on the streets in sheep's clothing."

"Be answerable to your friend who stares at you , whenever you stand before a mirror."

"Truth often is not about what we see as truth , rather its what we don't see , that is ."

"More than prosperity, life is all about satiety."

41

"Losing hopes in life is perhaps your actual defeat, prior to the defeat that happens later."

"God's love is like layers of soothing balm over your tortured forehead."

"One day SHE will rise from the debris to conquer the world again."

"You are the soul author of the book of your life."

"When you are not conscious of your goodness, it tends to shine most ."

42

"Malice may burn your soul in a terrible fire of depravity,
where good advice may save it."

"Fly away like time , into the window of Future ,out through
the window of Present and taste the realm of glorious
Timelessness."

"Human mind is like an embroidery work, beautiful , despite
many knots it holds at its back."

"Surpass the edges of time , open the pandora box that you are."

Thank You For Reading!

Hope the contents of the book have touched your heart and ignited a fire of motivation in your own life. Your response to my expressions can be best acknowledged if you take life as it comes to you and have firm faith in the Almighty. On a positive note, that after every failure comes success, I offer my thanks to you all!

With your blessings and support I would love to publish more for your reading. If you want to give me a feedback about this book then you can e-mail me on : smitabakshi02@gmail.com.

If you liked this book of mine, do read the first one, that is my book - 'DAWN TO DUSK (A Plethora Of Poems)'.

Enter Caption